30036011089974

S0-AYO-319

Pebble® Plus

Cool Sports Facts

Cool Basketball Facts

by Abby Czeskleba

Consulting Editor: Gail Saunders-Smith, PhD

Consultant: Craig Coenen, PhD
Associate Professor of History
Mercer County Community College
West Windsor, New Jersey

CAPSTONE PRESS
a capstone imprint

Pebble Plus is published by Capstone Press,
151 Good Counsel Drive, P.O. Box 669, Mankato, Minnesota 56002.
www.capstonepub.com

Books published by Capstone Press are manufactured with paper
containing at least 10 percent post-consumer waste.

Library of Congress Cataloging-in-Publication Data
Czeskleba, Abby.
  Cool basketball facts / by Abby Czeskleba.
    p. cm.—(Pebble plus. Cool sports facts)
  Includes bibliographical references and index.
  Summary: "Simple text and full-color photos illustrate facts about the rules, equipment, and records of basketball"—
Provided by publisher.
  ISBN 978-1-4296-4478-5 (library binding)
  ISBN 978-1-4296-7380-8 (paperback)
  1. Basketball—Miscellanea—Juvenile literature. I. Title. II. Series.

GV885.1.C94 2011
796.323—dc22   2009051409

Editorial Credits
Erika L. Shores, editor; Kyle Grenz, designer; Eric Gohl, media researcher; Eric Manske, production specialist

Photo Credits
Comstock Images, cover (basketball), back cover, 1
Dreamstime/Mike Liu, cover
NBAE via Getty Images Inc./David Liam Kyle, 5; Dick Raphael, 7; Jesse D. Garrabrant, 13, 21; Lisa Blumenfeld, 15;
    Melissa Majchrzak, 11; Nathaniel S. Butler, 19; Noah Graham, 17
Newscom/Icon SMI/Albert Pena, 9

Note to Parents and Teachers

The Cool Sports Facts series supports national social studies standards related to people, places,
and culture. This book describes and illustrates basketball. The images support early readers
in understanding the text. The repetition of words and phrases helps early readers learn new
words. This book also introduces early readers to subject-specific vocabulary words, which are
defined in the Glossary section. Early readers may need assistance to read some words and to
use the Table of Contents, Glossary, Read More, Internet Sites, and Index sections of the book.

Printed in the United States of America in North Mankato, Minnesota.
032011   006110CGF11

Table of Contents

Slam Dunk!

Each year, NBA players slam dunk in front of 21 million fans.

In 2009, players dunked more than 9,000 times.

NBA stands for National Basketball Association.

Cool Equipment

In 1985, Michael Jordan wore different shoes than his teammates. He broke NBA rules. The NBA fined him $5,000 for each game.

Michael Jordan

Teams get six basketballs
to use during warm-ups
before a game.
The number of balls is listed
in the NBA rule book.

Cool Rules

A team with the basketball

has 24 seconds to take a shot.

A player must shoot

a free throw within

10 seconds.

shot clock

It's against the rules

to kick the ball on purpose.

Kicking the ball into the stands

gets the player kicked out

of the game.

Cool Records

The Women's National

Basketball Association

began in 1997.

Lisa Leslie scored

the first dunk in the WNBA.

In 2008, Jordan Farmar set
a dribbling record.
At the NBA All-Star Jam
Session, Farmar dribbled
a ball 228 times in one minute.

NBA star Robert Parish played in 1,611 NBA games. No one has played more NBA games than he has.

The Boston Celtics have won
the most NBA championships
with 17. They won 11
of these championships
in just 13 years.

NBA FINALS CHAMPION
COVIDIEN
Banknorth
OF HOCKEY
NESN HD
DUNKIN' DO
BOSTON
BOSTON
2008 NBA CHAMPIONS
CHAMPIONS

Glossary

dribble—to bounce a basketball off the floor using one hand

dunk—when a player jumps above the basketball rim with the basketball and throws it in the net

fine—to charge someone money for breaking a rule

free throw—a shot taken from the free-throw line by a player when the other team makes a foul

Read More

Franks, Katie. *I Want to Be a Basketball Player.* Dream Jobs. New York: PowerKids Press, 2007.

Ladewski, Paul. *Stars on the Court.* New York: Scholastic, 2009.

Internet Sites

FactHound offers a safe, fun way to find Internet sites related to this book. All of the sites on FactHound have been researched by our staff.

Here's all you do:

Visit *www.facthound.com*

FactHound will fetch the best sites for you!

Index

Word Count: 190
Grade: 1
Early-Intervention Level: 21